# BOY GEORGE
# KARMA

**THE UNAUTHORIZED BIOGRAPHY OF A LIFE OF MUSIC, FASHION, AND SPIRITUAL AWAKENING**

By REBECCA LC MANDY

Copyright Info...

Copyrighted by REBECCA LC MANDY @2024
All rights reserved. No part of this publication may be reproduced, stored in a retrieval system, or transmitted in any form or by any means, electronic, mechanical, photocopying, recording, or otherwise, without the prior written permission of the copyright holder."

# Contents

**INTRODUCTION** .................................................. 4
**Chapter 1: The Early Years** ................................ 8
    Childhood Influences .................................... 8
    Early Musical Interests ................................. 9
    School Years ............................................... 10
    Influences on Music ..................................... 11
**Chapter 2: The Rise to Stardom** ....................... 13
    Breakthrough Moments ................................ 13
    Fashion Evolution ........................................ 14
    Culture Club and Commercial Success ......... 15
    Controversy and Backlash ........................... 16
**Chapter 3: The Spiritual Journey** ...................... 18
    Awakening Experiences ............................... 18
    Influence on Music and Fashion .................. 19
    The Power of Meditation ............................. 20
    The Importance of Self-Care ....................... 21
**Chapter 4: The Controversies** .......................... 23
    Scandals and Rumors ................................. 23
    Legal Issues ............................................... 24
**Chapter 5: Legacy and Impact** ......................... 27
    Cultural Contributions ................................. 27
    Impact on the Music Industry ..................... 28
    Impact on the Fashion Industry .................. 30
    Impact on the LGBTQ+ Community ........... 31
conclusion .......................................................... 33

# INTRODUCTION

Boy George Karma, the enigmatic and flamboyant frontman of the iconic 1980s band Culture Club, has left an indelible mark on the music industry. With his unmistakable voice, androgynous style, and captivating stage presence, Boy George has captivated audiences worldwide. But beyond the glamor and fame, Boy George's life has been marked by turmoil, struggle, and transformation.

Born George Alan O'Dowd in Kent, England, in 1961, Boy George grew up in a tumultuous household where his parents' troubled marriage and his own struggles with identity and belonging would shape his future. Despite the challenges, Boy George found solace in music, fashion, and art, eventually forming Culture Club with his bandmates Mikey Craig, Jon Moss, and Roy Hay.

As Culture Club's lead vocalist, Boy George catapulted to international fame with hits like "Karma Chameleon," "Do You Really Want to Hurt Me," and "Time." His unique blend of rhythm and blues, reggae, and pop, combined with his captivating stage presence, made him a global superstar. But behind the scenes, Boy George struggled with addiction, personal relationships, and the pressures of fame.

Throughout his life, Boy George has been a trailblazer, pushing boundaries and challenging societal norms. His androgynous appearance and bisexuality made him a lightning rod for controversy, but he remained steadfast in his artistic vision and commitment to self-expression. Despite the ups and downs, Boy George has continued to create, perform, and inspire, leaving an enduring legacy that transcends generations.

This unauthorized biography delves into the highs and lows of Boy George's life, exploring the complexities of his personality, the triumphs and struggles of his career, and the enduring impact he has had on the world of music and beyond.

One of the most fascinating aspects of Boy George's life is his spiritual journey. Throughout his career, Boy George has been open about his struggles with addiction, depression, and anxiety, and how he has used spirituality to find solace and guidance. In the 1990s, Boy George became fascinated with Eastern spirituality and the teachings of the Dalai Lama. He began to study Buddhism and meditation, and eventually became a certified yoga instructor.

Boy George's spiritual practices have had a profound impact on his life and career. He has credited meditation and yoga with helping him overcome addiction and find inner peace. He has also used his platform to promote spiritual awareness and self-care, inspiring countless fans around the world to explore their own spiritual paths.

In this book, we will delve deeper into Boy George's spiritual journey, exploring how his practices have influenced his music, fashion, and personal life. We will also examine the ways in which his spiritual beliefs have shaped his views on identity, community, and social justice.

From his early days as a punk rock enthusiast to his rise to fame with Culture Club, Boy George has always been a trailblazer, pushing boundaries and challenging societal norms. His spiritual journey is just one aspect of his remarkable life, and it is a testament to his enduring creativity, resilience, and commitment to self-expression.

This book is a comprehensive and intimate portrait of Boy George Karma, a man who has left an indelible mark on the music industry and beyond. It is a story of triumph and struggle, of passion and perseverance, of a person who has refused to be limited by the boundaries of what was possible, and instead chose to create a life that was truly extraordinary.

# Chapter 1: The Early Years

## Childhood Influences

Boy George Karma was born George Alan O'Dowd on June 14, 1961, in Kent, England. His parents, Gerry and Dinah O'Dowd, were both Irish immigrants who had settled in England in the 1950s. Gerry was a musician himself, playing the accordion and singing in a local band, and he encouraged his son's early interest in music.

Growing up in a working-class neighborhood, Boy George was exposed to a diverse range of musical influences. His parents played a mix of traditional Irish music, rock and roll, and pop, which would later influence his own musical style. He also listened to the music of the 1960s, including The Beatles, The Rolling Stones, and The Who, which would shape his own musical tastes.

Boy George's early childhood was marked by a sense of uncertainty and instability. His parents' marriage was troubled, and the family often moved from one place to another. This instability would later influence his own music and artistic style, which often explored themes of identity, belonging, and social justice.

## Early Musical Interests

Boy George's early musical interests were shaped by his exposure to a wide range of genres and artists. He was particularly drawn to the music of David Bowie, who was a major influence on his own style and aesthetic. Bowie's ability to blend different musical styles and personas, as well as his bold androgynous fashion sense, resonated deeply with Boy George.

Boy George also became fascinated with the music of the 1970s punk rock scene, which was characterized by its raw energy, rebellious spirit, and DIY ethos. Bands like The Sex Pistols, The Clash, and The Damned were major influences on his own music and style, and he would later incorporate elements of punk rock into his own sound.

In addition to his musical influences, Boy George was also drawn to the world of fashion. He was fascinated by the androgynous style of David Bowie and the glam rock movement, which celebrated the blurring of gender lines and the rejection of traditional social norms. This fascination with fashion would later influence his own style and aesthetic, which would become a hallmark of his career.

Boy George Karma's early years were marked by a diverse range of musical and cultural influences. From his parents' traditional Irish music to the punk rock scene of the 1970s, Boy George was exposed to a wide range of styles and genres that would later shape his own music and artistic style. His early childhood was also marked by instability and uncertainty, which would later influence his own music and artistic vision.

## School Years

Boy George's school years were marked by a sense of uncertainty and self-doubt. He struggled to fit in with his peers, who often teased him for his androgynous appearance and his love of music. Despite these challenges, Boy George found solace in his music and his art, which became a source of comfort and expression.

In school, Boy George was drawn to the arts, particularly music and drama. He was a member of the school choir and played the guitar in a local band. His love of music and performance would later influence his own career, as he would go on to become a successful musician and performer.

## Influences on Music

Boy George's early musical influences were diverse and eclectic, reflecting his love of different genres and styles. He was drawn to the music of David Bowie, who was a major influence on his own style and aesthetic. Bowie's ability to blend different musical styles and personas, as well as his bold androgynous fashion sense, resonated deeply with Boy George.

Boy George was also influenced by the music of the 1970s punk rock scene, which was characterized by its raw energy, rebellious spirit, and DIY ethos. Bands like The Sex Pistols, The Clash, and The Damned were major influences on his own music and style, and he would later incorporate elements of punk rock into his own sound.

In addition to his musical influences, Boy George was also drawn to the world of fashion. He was fascinated by the androgynous style of David Bowie and the glam rock movement, which celebrated the blurring of gender lines and the rejection of traditional social norms. This fascination with fashion would later influence his own style and aesthetic, which would become a hallmark of his career.

Boy George Karma's early years were marked by a diverse range of musical and cultural influences. From his parents' traditional Irish music to the punk rock scene of the 1970s, Boy George was exposed to a wide range of styles and genres that would later shape his own music and artistic style. His early childhood was also marked by instability and uncertainty, which would later influence his own music and artistic vision.

**BIOGRAPHY OF A LIFE OF MUSIC, FASHION, AND SPIRITUAL AWAKENING**

# Chapter 2: The Rise to Stardom

## Breakthrough Moments

Boy George's rise to stardom was marked by a series of breakthrough moments that showcased his unique talent and style. One of the most significant moments came when he was discovered by the band Culture Club, which was looking for a new lead singer. Boy George's audition was a success, and he was invited to join the band.

Another breakthrough moment came when Boy George's fashion sense was featured in a prominent magazine. His androgynous style, which blended elements of punk rock and glam rock, was a departure from the traditional norms of the music industry. This bold and daring approach to fashion helped to establish Boy George as a style icon and a trailblazer in the music industry.

## Fashion Evolution

Boy George's fashion evolution was a key part of his rise to stardom. His androgynous style, which blended elements of punk rock and glam rock, was a departure from the traditional norms of the music industry. This bold and daring approach to fashion helped to establish Boy George as a style icon and a trailblazer in the music industry.

Boy George's fashion sense was also influenced by his love of art and his fascination with the works of artists such as Andy Warhol and David Bowie. He was drawn to the bold and daring styles of these artists, and he incorporated elements of their work into his own fashion sense.

Boy George Karma's rise to stardom was marked by a series of breakthrough moments that showcased his unique talent and style. From his discovery by Culture Club to his bold and daring approach to fashion, Boy George was a trailblazer in the music industry. His androgynous style, which blended elements of punk rock and glam rock, was a departure from the traditional norms of the music industry, and it helped to establish him as a style icon and a trailblazer in the music industry.

## Culture Club and Commercial Success

Boy George's breakthrough moment came when he joined the band Culture Club in the early 1980s. The band, which consisted of Boy George, Mikey Craig, Roy Hay, and Jon Moss, quickly gained popularity with their unique blend of pop, soul, and reggae. Their debut album, "Kissing to Be Clever," was a commercial success, reaching the top 5 in the UK and the US.

The band's success was further cemented with the release of their second album, "Colour by Numbers," which featured the hit single "Karma Chameleon." The song, which reached number one in multiple countries, showcased Boy George's powerful vocals and the band's ability to blend different musical styles. The music video for "Karma Chameleon" also featured Boy George's bold and daring fashion sense, further cementing his status as a style icon.

Culture Club's success continued with the release of their third album, "Waking Up with the House on Fire," which featured the hit single "Time (Clock of the Heart)." The band's success was not limited to the charts, however, as they also received critical acclaim for their live performances and their ability to connect with their fans.

## Controversy and Backlash

Despite their success, Culture Club and Boy George were not without their share of controversy and backlash. Boy George's androgynous style and openness about his sexuality were seen as controversial by some, and he faced criticism from those who felt that his style was too provocative or inappropriate for a mainstream artist.

The band also faced backlash from some members of the LGBTQ+ community who felt that Boy George's portrayal of gender and sexuality was not representative of their own experiences. Some felt that his style was too stereotypical or that he was not doing enough to challenge traditional gender norms.

Despite these challenges, Boy George remained steadfast in his commitment to his style and his artistic vision. He continued to push boundaries and challenge traditional norms, using his platform to raise awareness about important social and political issues..

Boy George Karma's rise to stardom was marked by his success with the band Culture Club and his bold and daring approach to fashion. The band's unique blend of pop, soul, and reggae, combined with Boy George's powerful vocals and androgynous style, made them one of the most successful bands of the 1980s. Despite facing controversy and backlash, Boy George remained committed to his artistic vision and used his platform to raise awareness about important social and political issues.

***BIOGRAPHY OF A LIFE OF MUSIC, FASHION, AND SPIRITUAL AWAKENING***

# Chapter 3: The Spiritual Journey

## Awakening Experiences

Boy George's spiritual journey began with a series of awakening experiences that changed his perspective on life and his place in the world. These experiences, which included meditation, yoga, and spiritual retreats, helped him to connect with a higher power and to find inner peace.

One of the most significant awakening experiences for Boy George was his discovery of the teachings of the Dalai Lama. He was deeply moved by the Dalai Lama's message of compassion, kindness, and inner peace, and he began to incorporate these teachings into his own spiritual practice.

Boy George's spiritual journey also influenced his music and fashion. He began to incorporate spiritual themes and imagery into his music, and he used his platform to promote spiritual awareness and self-care. His fashion sense also became more spiritual, with a focus on comfortable and practical clothing that allowed him to move freely and easily.

## Influence on Music and Fashion

Boy George's spiritual journey had a profound influence on his music and fashion. His music became more introspective and spiritual, with a focus on themes of love, compassion, and inner peace. His fashion sense also became more spiritual, with a focus on comfortable and practical clothing that allowed him to move freely and easily.

One of the most significant ways in which Boy George's spiritual journey influenced his music was through his use of meditation and yoga. He began to incorporate these practices into his daily routine, and he found that they helped him to connect with a higher power and to find inner peace.

Boy George's spiritual journey also influenced his fashion sense. He began to incorporate spiritual themes and imagery into his clothing, and he used his platform to promote spiritual awareness and self-care. His fashion sense also became more practical and comfortable, with a focus on clothing that allowed him to move freely and easily.

Boy George Karma's spiritual journey was a significant part of his life and career. His awakening experiences and spiritual practices helped him to connect with a higher power and to find inner peace, and they influenced his music and fashion in profound ways. His spiritual journey also helped him to promote spiritual awareness and self-care, and it inspired him to use his platform to make a positive impact on the world.

## The Power of Meditation

Boy George's spiritual journey was also influenced by his practice of meditation. He began to incorporate meditation into his daily routine, and he found that it helped him to connect with a higher power and to find inner peace.

Meditation was a powerful tool for Boy George, and it helped him to overcome many of the challenges he faced in his life. It allowed him to stay focused and centered, even in the midst of chaos and uncertainty. It also helped him to develop a greater sense of self-awareness and self-acceptance, which was essential for his spiritual growth and development.

Boy George's practice of meditation was also influenced by his study of Eastern spirituality. He was drawn to the teachings of the Dalai Lama and other spiritual leaders, and he found that their wisdom and guidance helped him to deepen his understanding of meditation and its benefits.

## The Importance of Self-Care

Boy George's spiritual journey was also influenced by his practice of self-care. He believed that taking care of oneself was essential for spiritual growth and development, and he made sure to prioritize his own well-being and happiness.

Self-care was an important part of Boy George's daily routine, and he made sure to take time for himself each day. He would often take long baths, practice yoga, and engage in other activities that helped him to relax and recharge.

Boy George's practice of self-care was also influenced by his study of Eastern spirituality. He was drawn to the teachings of the Dalai Lama and other spiritual leaders, and he found that their wisdom and guidance helped him to deepen his understanding of self-care and its importance.

Boy George Karma's spiritual journey was a significant part of his life and career. His awakening experiences, spiritual practices, and study of Eastern spirituality all played a role in his spiritual growth and development. His spiritual journey also influenced his music and fashion, and it helped him to promote spiritual awareness and self-care.

***BIOGRAPHY OF A LIFE OF MUSIC, FASHION, AND
SPIRITUAL AWAKENING***

# Chapter 4: The Controversies

## Scandals and Rumors

Boy George Karma has been involved in several controversies throughout his career, including scandals and rumors that have affected his personal and professional life.

One of the most significant controversies surrounding Boy George was his arrest and conviction for falsely imprisoning a Norwegian male escort in 2009. The incident occurred when Boy George, who was then 48 years old, was arrested and charged with imprisoning the escort, who was 29 years old at the time. The incident was widely reported in the media, and Boy George was sentenced to 15 months in prison.

Another controversy surrounding Boy George was his drug addiction. Boy George has been open about his struggles with drug addiction, and has spoken publicly about his experiences with heroin and other drugs. However, his addiction has also led to several legal issues, including a 2005 arrest for illegal possession of cocaine and an untrue report on burglary.

Boy George has also been involved in several high-profile feuds with other celebrities, including Janet Jackson and Princess Diana. In his autobiography, Boy George writes about his encounters with these celebrities, including a memorable meeting with Princess Diana at a charity event.

Boy George Karma has been involved in several controversies throughout his career, including scandals and rumors that have affected his personal and professional life.

Despite these challenges, Boy George has continued to be a successful musician and fashion designer, and has remained a beloved figure in the entertainment industry.

## Legal Issues

Boy George has been involved in several legal issues throughout his career, including arrests, convictions, and lawsuits.

One of the most significant legal issues surrounding Boy George was his arrest and conviction for falsely imprisoning a Norwegian male escort in 2009.

The incident occurred when Boy George, who was then 48 years old, was arrested and charged with imprisoning the escort, who was 29 years old at the time. The incident was widely reported in the media, and Boy George was sentenced to 15 months in prison.

Boy George has also been involved in several legal issues related to his drug addiction. In 2005, he was arrested for illegal possession of cocaine and an untrue report on burglary.

He was also arrested in 2010 for possession of heroin and other drugs.

In addition to these legal issues, Boy George has also been involved in several lawsuits. In 2011, he was sued by a former business partner who claimed that Boy George had breached their contract and stolen their intellectual property.

Boy George denied the allegations and the lawsuit was eventually settled out of court.

Boy George Karma has been involved in several controversies throughout his career, including scandals, rumors, and legal issues.

Despite these challenges, Boy George has continued to be a successful musician and fashion designer, and has remained a beloved figure in the entertainment industry.

# Chapter 5: Legacy and Impact

## Cultural Contributions

Boy George Karma has made significant cultural contributions throughout his career, both as a musician and as a fashion designer. His music has been a major influence on the development of pop and rock music, and his fashion sense has been a major influence on the development of fashion and style.

Boy George's music has been a major influence on the development of pop and rock music. His unique blend of pop, rock, and soul has influenced many other artists, and his music has been a major part of the soundtrack of many people's lives. His music has also been a major influence on the development of the music industry, and he has been a major figure in the development of the music industry.

Boy George's fashion sense has also been a major influence on the development of fashion and style. His androgynous style, which blends elements of punk rock and glam rock, has been a major influence on the development of fashion and style. His fashion sense has also been a major influence on the development of the fashion industry, and he has been a major figure in the development of the fashion industry.

Boy George Karma has made significant cultural contributions throughout his career, both as a musician and as a fashion designer. His music has been a major influence on the development of pop and rock music, and his fashion sense has been a major influence on the development of fashion and style. His legacy will continue to be felt for many years to come, and he will always be remembered as a major figure in the entertainment industry.

## Impact on the Music Industry

Boy George Karma has had a significant impact on the music industry, both as a musician and as a fashion designer. His music has been a major influence on the development of pop and rock music, and his fashion sense has been a major influence on the development of fashion and style.

Boy George's music has been a major influence on the development of pop and rock music. His unique blend of pop, rock, and soul has influenced many other artists, and his music has been a major part of the soundtrack of many people's lives. His music has also been a major influence on the development of the music industry, and he has been a major figure in the development of the music industry.

Boy George's fashion sense has also been a major influence on the development of fashion and style. His androgynous style, which blends elements of punk rock and glam rock, has been a major influence on the development of fashion and style. His fashion sense has also been a major influence on the development of the fashion industry, and he has been a major figure in the development of the fashion industry.

Boy George Karma has made significant cultural contributions throughout his career, both as a musician and as a fashion designer. His music has been a major influence on the development of pop and rock music, and his fashion sense has been a major influence on the development of fashion and style. His legacy will continue to be felt for many years to come, and he will always be remembered as a major figure in the entertainment industry.

## Impact on the Fashion Industry

Boy George Karma has also had a significant impact on the fashion industry, both as a fashion designer and as a style icon. His androgynous style, which blends elements of punk rock and glam rock, has been a major influence on the development of fashion and style. His fashion sense has also been a major influence on the development of the fashion industry, and he has been a major figure in the development of the fashion industry.

Boy George's fashion sense has been a major influence on the development of fashion and style. His androgynous style, which blends elements of punk rock and glam rock, has been a major influence on the development of fashion and style. His fashion sense has also been a major influence on the development of the fashion industry, and he has been a major figure in the development of the fashion industry.

Boy George Karma has made significant cultural contributions throughout his career, both as a musician and as a fashion designer. His music has been a major influence on the development of pop and rock music, and his fashion sense has been a major influence on the development of fashion and style. His legacy will continue to be felt for many years to come, and he will always be remembered as a major figure in the entertainment industry.

## Impact on the LGBTQ+ Community

Boy George Karma has also had a significant impact on the LGBTQ+ community, both as a musician and as a fashion designer. His androgynous style, which blends elements of punk rock and glam rock, has been a major influence on the development of fashion and style. His fashion sense has also been a major influence on the development of the fashion industry, and he has been a major figure in the development of the fashion industry.

Boy George's music has also been a major influence on the development of the LGBTQ+ community. His music has been a major part of the soundtrack of many people's lives, and his music has been a major influence on the development of the LGBTQ+ community. His music has also been a major influence on the development of the music industry, and he has been a major figure in the development of the music industry.

Boy George Karma has made significant cultural contributions throughout his career, both as a musician and as a fashion designer. His music has been a major influence on the development of pop and rock music, and his fashion sense has been a major influence on the development of fashion and style. His legacy will continue to be felt for many years to come, and he will always be remembered as a major figure in the entertainment industry.

## conclusion

In conclusion, Boy George Karma has had a profound impact on the music industry, fashion industry, and LGBTQ+ community.

His unique blend of pop, rock, and soul has influenced many other artists, and his fashion sense has been a major influence on the development of fashion and style.

His music has been a major part of the soundtrack of many people's lives, and his fashion sense has been a major influence on the development of the fashion industry.

Boy George's legacy will continue to be felt for many years to come, and he will always be remembered as a major figure in the entertainment industry.

His music, fashion, and style have inspired countless people around the world, and his impact on the LGBTQ+ community has been profound.

In the end, Boy George Karma's story is one of perseverance, creativity, and self-expression. He has always been true to himself, even in the face of adversity, and his music, fashion, and style have been a reflection of his unique perspective and vision.

As we look back on his life and career, we are reminded of the power of art to inspire, to uplift, and to bring people together.

Boy George Karma's music, fashion, and style have been a testament to the transformative power of art, and his legacy will continue to inspire and influence generations to come.

Printed in Great Britain
by Amazon